Gary Jones

Florence

Contents

1

FLORENCE INTRODUCTION

Florence has a rich history with a strong artistic significance.The city is home to many valuable artworks from its stunning cathedrals, charming cobbled stones, maze of alleys, impressive architecture, breathtaking frescoes, priceless sculptures and paintings. This city is a beauty beyond compare.

From the museums and galleries, to the fashion, coffee and food, Florence promises an unforgettable adventure. With the help of this book, you can have a truly beautiful experience as we show you the best museums and galleries to explore, the best Piazzas to hang out, the best foods to eat, the most interesting activities, the best coffee to taste and the most affordable hotels to stay at.

If you want to have the best of everything in Florence, then you picked out the right book. Are you ready for a new adventure? Are you ready to create beautiful memories that will last a lifetime? If you are, then you are ready for this book.

I hope you enjoy it!

2

A Brief History of Florence

BELLA FIRENZE

A Brief History of Florence

What was Florence before it became the birthplace of the Renaissance?

Julius Caesar, who founded the city in 59 BC, called it Florentina, which means "flourishing." It was a military camp, but it indeed flourished to a commercial center because of its excellent location and fertile land. It was destroyed by the 4th century because of the war between German Ostrogoths and Byzantines.

Florence rose from the destruction and slowly restored under the Lombards. The city continued to prosper under Charlemagne's rule in 774. It proved to be stronger amidst the political strife during the 14th century. In 1252, Florence started to mint florin, the city's own gold currency.

Soon enough, it turned to a banking hub with the Medici family running the city behind the scenes. Because of their access to wealth, the Medici family became a strong influence in the arts scene. They were among the prominent art patrons Florence has ever seen.

The Birth of the Renaissance

Florence led the way to creative movement and innovation. Plenty of artist's guilds grew all over the city. The great masters Michelangelo, Botticelli, Ghirlandaio and Leonardo da Vinci emerged. They spread their masterpieces throughout the city, created valuable paintings, sculptures, and frescoes and greatly improved the city's architecture.

The City and the Medici

The Medici family continued to demonstrate a strong influence in politics until 1527 when the history about Florence they commissioned for Niccolo Machiavelli was published. It revealed their activities. The Florentine government made a concerted effort to expel the influential family. The republic was re-established.

The Medici's however, were not willing to give up without a fight. They made attempts in an effort to regain power. In 1537, they were declared as hereditary dukes of the city. By 1569, the Medici's became Tuscany's Grand Dukes and so they continued to rule for the next two centuries.

Florence and Italy

It was not long until Austria took over Tuscany. Florence was passed over to France then to the Kingdom of Sardinia-Piedmont. By 1861, Tuscany was joined to the Kingdom of Italy as one of its provinces. It even became the capital. Italy's first parliament was hosted at Florence. In 1871 however, Florence was replaced by Rome.

Florence Today

The City is still a thriving banking hub. Thanks to the great contributions of artists with support from the Medici's, Florence is known all over the world because of its strong artistic and historical significance. The city's great character among other things is what attracts people all over the world to experience this great city.

Get Your Free eBook At The End of The Book !!

3

Transport and Safety

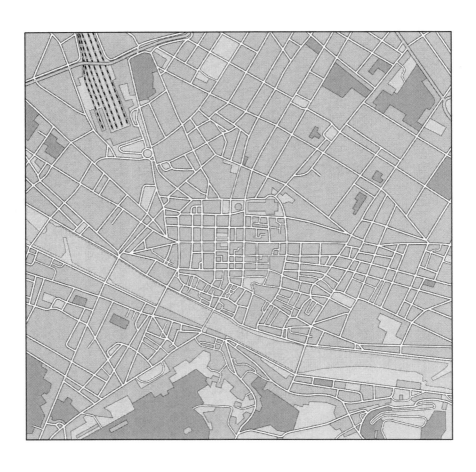

BUON VIAGGIO!

Transport and Safety

Arriving in Florence is your first step.If you are flying, you will arrive at the international airport in Florence.You will have several options to get from the airport to Florence.

Click Here For Transport Options From The Airport
http://www.aeroporto.firenze.it/en/
the-passengers/transport.html
Airport Map
https://goo.gl/maps/WUzdyJnxY4S2
Phone:+39 055 30615

Getting Around Florence

Getting around Florence is easy even if you are a tourist. That's because you can get from one major attraction to another on foot. Buy a map that points out the major attractions you want to visit and you're good to go.

If you don't like to walk, you can also avail of public transportation to take you around this beautiful city. The city bus, for example, is a good option. Here are your transport options.

Bus

The public buses in Florentine are run by ATAF. Tickets are sold at bars, newsstands, kiosks and the bus station, which is located outside the train station at Santa Maria Novella. When you see the sign, "Biglietti ATAF" in an establishment around the city, you are likely to buy a ticket there.

You can also buy a ticket from the bus driver himself, but it will cost you €2 more than when you buy it outside at €1.20 for a single ticket. One day ticket will cost you €5 while a 4-ride ticket is sold at €4.50. In Florence, bus tickets are either swiped or stamps depending on the type of ticket you get. You can avail of the bus transport system from 7am to 8:30 or around 9pm daily.

Phone:800424500

Bus Website
http://www.ataf.net/en/ataf.aspx?idC=2&LN=en-US

Bicycle and Scooter

You can also tour the city by bicycle or scooter. There are several bike rental shops around. There are plenty in the North of Piazza San Marco. You can also rent vintage-style bikes for €2.50 per hour or €12 per day. Mountain bikes are also available for €3 per hour or €18 per day. 100cc scooters are rented out for €15 per hour or €55 per day.

Address:Via S. Zanobi, 54R
Phone:+39 055 488992
Bicycle Website
http://www.florencebybike.it/en/about-us/
Bicycle Map
https://goo.gl/maps/n6XPpLKwimS2

Address:Via Il Prato, 50Rosso, 50123 Firenze
Phone:+39 055 538 5045
Scooter and Bike Website
http://www.vesparental.eu/index.php/en/
Scooter and Bike Map
https://goo.gl/maps/5bjb1sAHozq

Taxi

In Florence, people don't hail cabs from the streets. Instead, you can call for a cab by phone or wait for one at the taxi stand. There's a taxi stand at the main train station.

There are some spread out in squares and other popular tourist spots. Ask your hotel concierge for reliable taxi operators or request to call one in your behalf if you're coming from the hotel. A word of advice, because taxi fare in Florence is expensive, avoid taking one unless you really need to. Here's to give you an idea on how expensive taxis can be. The minimum taxi fare is €3.30 plus €0.91 per kilometer with additional €1 per bag.

Phone:055 4390
Taxi Website
http://www.4390.it/wp/contatti

Car

Driving is not recommended when you're touring Florence. If you are not used to narrow streets, do not even dare. Plus, a lot of drivers don't respect the traffic rules so you'll only be asking for trouble if you dare drive a rental in and around Florence.

Car parking is another problem. Because the city center is quite busy, you will have a hard time finding a parking spot. Cars are only recommended if you are taking a trip outside the city center. Otherwise, it is not practical.

Address:Borgo Ognissanti, 128
Phone:+39 055 213629
Car Map
https://goo.gl/maps/MVfC23Qzh6M2

Train

The main train station is found at the historic old town's edge along Santa Maria Novella.

You can take either the express or local trains to get to other parts of the country. The Eurostar trains particularly, can take you from Florence to other major cities of Italy or to other European countries.

Phone:1-877-375-7245
Email: info@italiarail.com
Train Website
https://www.italiarail.com/

Address:Stazione Ferroviaria,
Piazza Santa Maria Novella
Phone:+39 055 235 2595
Florence Train Station Website
http://www.firenzesantamarianovella.it/it/
Florence Train Station Map
https://goo.gl/maps/QFqVLCqq6C72

Travelling Safely in Florence

Traveling is exciting but there's also a hint of worry about putting yourself in a foreign land at the mercy of the locals. To put your mind at ease, the city of Florence is generally safe. However, this does not mean you should put your guard down.

Understand that any major city in any country will have a few problems regarding snatchers, pickpockets, and panhandlers. These crooks usually hang out in the most crowded tourist areas and even at train stations. How will you protect yourself against petty crimes and other possible dangers? Here are a couple of suggestions:

Secure your valuables.

The hotel provides a safe for a good reason. Use it to store your valuables. When you go out around the city for a tour, take only what you need. Wear your wallet securely. Hide your wallet where it cannot be easily reached by pickpockets. Wearing a neck pouch or a money belt may be a good idea.

Avoid putting all your eggs in one basket.

You can either leave your important documents securely locked in the safe or put them in a separate storage from your cash and your cards. Have a separate wallet for your cards, coins, and paper bills. Store all important numbers on your phone and write them down on a piece of paper too. In case your phone is taken from you, you still have access to the numbers to call for help.

Avoid taking side streets.

Taking shortcuts may seem like a good idea but it won't be if you get cornered by crooks. The side streets may be safe during the day but at night, they can be dangerous. Take well-lit roads even if it means taking longer to get to your destination.

Wear appropriate clothing.

If you're visiting the place during the summer, be warned that the temperature can get really high and uncomfortable. Protect yourself by wearing sunscreen or sun hat. In fact, the sun can shine too hot even during spring and fall. Since you will be exposing yourself to the heat when you stroll by the Arno or the outlying churches and sit at an outdoor café, you need to protect your skin.

Wear comfortable but still appropriate clothing. If you are a woman, be wary of this. If you are showing off your legs on shorts or skirts, make sure you are covered up on top and vice versa. Here, showing too much skin will attract unwanted attention.

Florence is known for its lovely cobbled streets and piazzas. The sidewalks are unforgiving. In which case, it is a smart idea to wear comfortable footwear when you're touring.

Wear insect repellant.

Summer evenings in Florence can be a problem with mosquitoes flying around. If you're going out in the night, protect yourself with an insect repellent. You can also wear a slight sweater. It will help protect you further from mosquito bites. Pack lightly when you stroll around the city.

Bring your own supply.

If you take prescription medications, make sure you have enough to last for the entire trip. Pharmacies in Florence can be easily identified with a red or green cross. The problem is their medicines usually have different brand names. It can lead to a mix-up. To avoid problems, you should bring your own supply.

You also need to remember a few important emergency numbers. If you need immediate medical attention, the ambulance number is 118. If you need help, call the police at 112 or 113.

Just to clarify, Florence is not a dangerous place. The knowledge of petty crimes should not deter you from enjoying your trip. There are police officers around the city. Some are dispatched to protect tourists at the city's major attractions. These things are just for precautionary measures.

4

Areas of Florence and Best Time to Visit

IRENZE AVVENTURA

Areas of Florence and Best Time to Visit

To avoid misadventures in Florence, it is useful to familiarize yourself with the key areas of the city. We will provide you with a brief background of each and the things you can see there.

Duomo

This is probably where most of the hotels are found. There are plenty of eating places here too. That said, you have to be picky with both hotel and food options if you are buying what Duomo offers.

Among the oldest parts of Florence, Duomo is the area that surrounds the city's cathedrals. It is sandwiched between the monastic churches of Santa Croce and Santa Maria Novella. It is also in the middle of Ponte Vecchio and Uffizi Gallery in the south. In the North side, it is halfway between Michelangelo's David and the Accademia. In other words, it's the most central part of the city. If you take the maze of alleys of Duomo to the South, it will lead you to the Piazza Della Signoria.

Duomo Map
https://goo.gl/maps/CxgqoTogB2s

Oltrarno, San Niccolò and San Frediano

Oltrarno used to be known as the working-class neighborhood until it fell to the hands of the aristocrats and used it for building their palaces including the Pitti Palace. This palace was the home of grand dukes. Today, you will still see traces of the past although the Pitti Palace is now the home of paintings. It houses a wide scope of artworks but it is only second to Uffizi. You will also find a line of workshops in

Oltrarno as it is now the artisan's neighborhood.

Oltrarno's center, Piazza Santo Spirito, is shaded by trees. It is as lively at day as it is by night. Here is where you will find bars and plenty of great restaurants. To the west is the most fashionable neighborhood, the San Frediano. This area of Florence is not ideal for hotel accommodation. The neighborhood is excellent but the hotel price ranges are not favorable. The prices of food and drinks however, are much better than anywhere around the city.

Oltrarno Map
https://goo.gl/maps/ieZAAAYz5L82

San Niccolò Map
https://goo.gl/maps/JLzZJMcpr3A2

San Frediano Map
https://goo.gl/maps/KKWieeSk8Dv

Piazza della Signoria

Know this neighborhood as the museum area. It is where the Bargello sculpture collection and the Uffizi Gallery are found. It is also close to Ponte Vecchio that leads to the Pitti Palace.

Today, this area is a well-polished tourist zone. However, the city has maintained the charm of the narrow medieval streets, the same area where Dante spent time growing up.

To the North of Ponte Vecchio are modern but unappealing buildings. You may find them appealing though because this is the spot for bargain shopping. This area is severely crowded during the peak seasons. There are dining places here too. However, you should be selective about the restaurant to go to even if you are just craving for some gelato. This is not the right place for a food adventure.

Piazza della Signoria Map
https://goo.gl/maps/rHt6ePo7j6L2

Piazza Santa Trínita

This upscale but still medieval neighborhood is the home of haute couture. Found north of the river at the south of the city, Piazza Santa Trínita is the shopping mecca where you will find Armani, Gucci, Cavalli, etc.

Piazza Santa Trínita Map
https://goo.gl/maps/czquR2USD5Q2

San Lorenzo and the Mercato Centrale

Halfway between the Duomo and the train station, San Lorenzo is the market neighborhood. This is where you should head out to for various goods from food to leather to tourist wares. It is home to a large indoor food market.

San Lorenzo is a colorful neighborhood. It houses affordable restaurants and hotels. While it is where Michelangelo-designed tombs and the San Lorenzo church are found, it is far from being quiet. It is a busy neighborhood.

San Lorenzo Map
https://goo.gl/maps/a3W5z3MsJg92
Mercato Centrale Map
https://goo.gl/maps/mH3iXEQkZsC2

San Marco and Santissima Annunziata

While the Piazza San Marco is known for being a transport hub, Piazza Santissima Annunziata is regarded as Florence's most architecturally unified square. This neighborhood is home to the Accademia and Florence University. It also houses Fra' Angelico's San Marco paintings.

The streets are quieter in this area. It is where you are likely to find hotel gems. It is not too far from the main city center but it definitely provides a peaceful solace from the business of the crowds in nearby areas.

San Marco Map
https://goo.gl/maps/1RcEyokXe5q

Santissima Annunziata Map
https://goo.gl/maps/pvh7p55KGhB2

Santa Croce

It is the most genuine neighborhood in Florence. It has a pure local feel to it. This is the area of Florence where you will find some of the liveliest bars that offer the best aperitivos and the most exquisite restaurants worth exploring. There seems to be something exciting always happening especially along Via de' Benci, Via de' Macci and Via Panisperna.

Santa Croce Map
https://goo.gl/maps/grs5ZUNm4Go

Santa Maria Novella

Found at the western edge, Santa Maria Novella has two sides. The south side between the river and the church is quite pleasant. The other side however, located around the train station is probably the least attractive in all of Florence. As a tourist, it is best to avoid it and you would be wise not to book a hotel in the area.

Via Nazionale is always clogged in traffic. This side of the neighborhood is noisy. It is devoid of medieval feel to it. However, the good thing about the area is the bargain. Via Faenza is where most affordable budget options are to be found.

Santa Maria Novella Map
https://goo.gl/maps/VKVDVw6Z9Vq

So when is the best time to take a trip to Florence?

The best time depends on what you want to see and what you budget can tolerate. Tourists flock in between May and September because Florence is most vibrant during the summer. The city holds several events and endless activities for everyone to enjoy.

On the downside, all the prices are up, not to mention the hot temperature which can reach the upper 80s as well as the heavy foot traffic. If you want to have the perks of a summer trip without overspending, it is advisable to book a flight, hotel and museum tickets several months before your scheduled trip.

The months before and after the high peak season are also good especially for scoring the best hotel deals. In April, the sun shines bright with a fairer temperature at 45 to 65 degree Fahrenheit range. Great deals on hotels and less crowded. The downside is there are bigger chances of rain showers, which may dampen your touring spirit.

The sweetest spot of the year is October. You'll experience mild weather. This time of the year, Florence is less crowded than in the summer. And as the tourist flow slows down, you have a good chance of excellent deals. The downside is you have just missed out on the city's biggest events.

5

The Best Museums in Florence

SCOPRI FIRENZE

The Best Museums in Florence

Florence is a beautiful epitome of the Renaissance era. The city itself feels like a museum. Renaissance masterpieces are everywhere. Deep in the city are world-class museums that house valuable and priceless art works. Every single one of these museums is worth the time to explore. However, which ones are at the top of the list? We are counting down the best treasures of this Renaissance city from the most popular to the lesser known but equally interesting museums.

Museo Storico Topografico di Firenze com'era (Museum of "Florence as it was")

If you want to get to know the city, it is important to try to understand its past which is why it makes sense to visit this museum first. By taking a glimpse at how the city was, you will also have a much better appreciation of what it is today.

The museum remains in its original location since 1956, at the Oblate Sisters convent. Among the things you will find in this museum are the plans, etchings and paintings that speak of the history as well as the former appearance of Florence. There are many interesting things to see but the most extraordinary ones are the 'della cantena' plan. This is only a reproduction since the original is preserved at Berlin's Friedrich Museum.

The oil paintings demonstrate typical scenes of the 18th and 19th century Florence. They also represent some of the most notable historical events. The lunettes created by Giusto Utens in 1599, which he dedicated to the Medici villas are worth a closer look. The museum also showcases a Giuseppe Zocchi's collection of etchings dedicated to

Florentine villas, palaces and churches.

There is an entire section that houses Giuseppe Poggi's works. He was a Florentine town planner and architect. His works demonstrate Florence's transformation after 1865.

Address:Via dell'Oriuolo, 24
Phone:+39 055 261 6545
Museo Storico Topografico di Firenze com'era Map
https://goo.gl/maps/n2DFXoGEEHH2

Museo Nazionale del Bargello
(National Museum of Bargello)

This museum, which dates back to 1865, has the most extensive collection of sculptures from Michelangelo, Donatello, Cellini, Verrocchio and Luca della Robbia, among many others. It is found in what used to be the Palazzo del Popolo or the Palace of the Captain of the People along Via del Proconsolo. The palace dates back all the way to 1255. Among the main attractions of the museum are Michelangelo's masterpieces including Madonna and Child, David-Apollo, Bacchus and Brutus.

The National Museum of Bargello is open from Tuesday to Sunday as well as the 1st, 3rd and 5th Monday of each month. The operating hours are between 8:15am and 6pm. The entry fee is €4 with additional fee for special exhibitions.

Address:Via del Proconsolo, 4
Phone:+39 055 238 8606
Museo Nazionale del Bargello Map
https://goo.gl/maps/juwHhqS7xRy

Museo dell'Opera del Duomo
(Museum of the Cathedral Works)

Aren't you curious about how the Duomo was built? This museum provides bits and pieces of its history. You will also find a lot of the original important pieces here from the Duomo. There is also a vast display of machines that were used in building the cathedral including those designed by Brunelleschi. The original drafts and plans along with the wooden model proposal.

The real Bronze panels that were casted by Ghiberti, gothic statues and the statue from Giotto's Bell Tower carved by various artists including Cennini, Bernardo, Donatello and Michelozzo. However, the main attractions of the museum include Michelangelo's Pieta and Donatello's The Magdalene.

This museum is found at the Piazza del Duomo and it is open from Monday to Saturday between 9am and 7:30pm and on Sunday from 9am to 1:45pm. The entry fee is €6.

Address:Piazza del Duomo, 9
Phone:+39 055 230 2885
Museo dell'Opera del Duomo Website
https://operaduomo.firenze.it/en
Museo dell'Opera del Duomo Map

Museo di Storia della Scienza (Museo Galileo)

There are 45 rooms in the museum. Among the best highlights include the art works from the beginning of Tuscan art and the paintings that marked the beginning of the Renaissance. Be at awe as you are greeted by masterpieces including Filippo Lippi's iconic "Madonna and Child," Sandro Boticelli's awe-inspiring "The Birth of Venus," the original paintings of Leonardo da Vinci, Michelangelo, Raphael and Andrea del Sarto, Titian, Albrecht Dürer, Pontormo, Giovanni Bellini and other great Renaissance artists.

The gallery is open on weekdays from 8:15am to 6:50pm. Come to the gallery early unless you will be waiting in line along with the rest of the crowd. Entry fees vary. For information, you can call 055 2388651.

Address:Piazzale degli Uffizi, 6
Phone:+39 055 23885
Galleria degli Uffizi Website
http://www.uffizi.com/
Galleria degli Uffizi Map

Galleria dell'Accademia
(Accademia Gallery)

Although its list of great artworks may not be as extensive or high profile as that of Uffizi's, Galleria dell'Accademia has one big thing that Uffizi doesn't have. It's Michelangelo's David. Next to Uffizi, it is the second most visited gallery in all of Florence.

Accademia Gallery also features various collections from Florentine Gothic and Renaissance era which includes the unfinished works of Michelangelo. The art gallery is open from Tuesday to Sunday between 8:15am and 6:30pm. The entry fee is €10.

Address:Via Ricasoli, 58/60
Phone:+39 055 238 8609
Galleria dell'Accademia Website
http://www.accademia.org/
Galleria dell'Accademia Map
https://goo.gl/maps/zdeabA1DzgC2

Galleria di Arte Moderna
(Gallery of Modern Art)

With great inspiration from the Renaissance, modern artists created their fare share of precious masterpieces, and you can find them at this art gallery. From the Neoclassics to the romantics to the historical, Galleria di Arte Moderna displays valuable art pieces. Among the must-sees include Giovanni Fattori's "Rotonda Palmieri," Silvestro Lega's "The Starling Song," Telemaco Signorini's "Leith." The gallery also features sculptures from the likes of Adriano Cecioni.

Located at Palazzo Pitti, the Gallery of Modern Art is open on Tuesdays to Sundays from 8:15am to 6:50pm. The full entry fee is €8.50.

Address:Piazza de' Pitti, 1
Phone:+39 055 238 8601
Galleria di Arte Moderna
https://goo.gl/maps/jPomGuJhvSp

7

The Best Coffee Shops in Florence

Posso avere una tazza di caffè?

The Best Coffee Shops in Florence

Florence has a lot more to offer than rich history and priceless masterpieces. The coffee shops and cafes are terrific, too. They are not only places where you can get a dose of caffeine boost after a long tour. They are not only a place where you can get a sweet slice of pastry to go with your coffee or tea. These coffee shops are social hubs and are very much part of the quintessential Italian culture.

Florence: Among the Best Places for Coffee

When the coffee culture started in Europe, coffee places were equivalent to elegance. People gathered in coffee shops not only to have a sip of the best refreshments but also to mingle. In Florence, grand cafes were where the intellectual and social elites gathered. A couple of these coffee places still stand today.

If you want a slice or a sip of true café culture, here is a list of the best coffee shops in the Renaissance city. Before we get to the list, here are a few clarifications. In Italy, caffe means espresso, latte is milk and caffe con latte is coffee with milk. Don't worry though since Florence is a tourist spot, you will surely find servers that can speak English. And now we proceed with the list.

Caffe Gilli

Established in 1733, the classically decorated Caffe Gilli is a hot tourist spot. They have mouthwatering pastries intricately displayed in a mile-long glass case. Their lively caffe has a hint of nuttiness with a touch of earthy flavors. The caffe goes well with the cream-filled profiteroles with a drizzle of satiny smooth chocolate ganache.

This caffe is located at the Piazza della Republica. It is expensive for a quick stop but the experience, the coffee, the grand interior and the heavenly chocolates may be worth it.

Address:Via Roma, 1/red
Phone:+39 055 213896
Caffe Gilli Website
https://www.facebook.com/CaffeGilli/
Caffe Gilli Map
https://goo.gl/maps/ojmTtrFmgJr

Caffe Paszkoswski

This is another old establishment founded in 1907. Caffe Paszkoswski is also located in the Piazza della Republica. It is a famous hangout for writers, musicians and artists. Needless to say, this caffe has a creative vibe. Their cappuccino although expensive, is quite inspiring.

Address:Piazza della Repubblica, 35/r
Phone:+39 055 210236
Caffe Paszkoswski Website
http://www.paszkowski.it/
Caffe Paszkoswski Map
https://goo.gl/maps/GvUGXCv9QNA2

Caffe Scudieri

Found within the Duomo, Caffe Scudieri offers among the best Tuscan-style espresso dolce. It has that milk chocolaty sweetness with a hint of toasted nut flavor. The caramel-smooth texture feels like heaven in the mouth. It also has one of the most luscious pastry offerings. Other things to try at the Caffe Scudieri include the velvety cappuccino, cream puffs and custardy fruit tart. It is a popular hangout for both locals and tourists.

Address:Piazza di San Giovanni, 19/R

Phone:+39 055 210733
Caffe Scudieri Website
http://www.scudieri.eu/info.html
Caffe Scudieri Map
https://goo.gl/maps/23L7cZ5pYNQ2

Caffe Giacosa

Found along Via Tournboni, Caffe Giacosa boasts of being the home of the best cappuccino in all of Florence. If you are familiar with the Italian cocktail Negroni, then you will be much delighted to know it came from this place. Designer Roberto Cavalli invested on Caffe Giacosa's restoration. Aside from the cappuccino, the historical features of Caffe Giacosa are another reason for you to drop by.

Address:Via della Spada, 10r
Phone:+39 055 277 6328
Caffe Giacosa Website
http://www.caffegiacosa.it/index.php?lang=en
Caffe Giacosa Map
https://goo.gl/maps/ACU2mvGTWAA2

La Loggia

This coffee shop is found along Via del Corso. La Loggia has a nice relaxing atmosphere. You can enjoy a full bodied coffee with a smooth finish. The most interesting thing about their caffe is that it has a citrus fruity flavor with a faint roasted note. The place also seems to have a continuous supply of freshly baked bombolini, an Italian filled donut.

Address:Piazzale Michelangelo, 1

Phone:+39 055 234 2832
La Loggia Website
http://www.ristorantelaloggia.it/
La Loggia Map
https://goo.gl/maps/bZSDDcgUacx

Arnold Coffee

If you like a more familiar ambience, Arnold Coffee does not disappoint. It is the equivalent of Starbucks in Florence. The pace of things is slow in this coffee place. It is a good place to hang out and relax. Coffee can be bought in three different sizes. The small size is served in Italian coffee cups. In addition, Arnold Coffee offers typical American cakes like cookies, bagels, wraps and donuts. This coffee shop is located in the neighborhood of Santa Maria Novella and you can access it through Piazza dell'Unità Italiana or Via degli Avelli.

Address:Via degli Avelli, 8
Phone:+39 055 906 0399
Arnold Coffee Website
http://www.arnoldcoffee.it/index.php?lang=en
Arnold Coffee Map
https://goo.gl/maps/HtfUGpJwU8B2

8

Best Bars and Nightclubs

La notte è appena cominciata, andiamo alla festa!

Best Bars and Nightclubs

Florence is not just about art, history, and culture. The Florentines also party hard! A night out in the city promises to be an exciting adventure. Here are a few suggestions to kick off an unforgettable night of great music, booze, and friendly company.

Kitsch

If you want to chill out and meet people, you can hang out at Kitsch where the vibe is casual and laid back. You are welcome to dinner which happens between 7pm and 10pm. You will be treated to an aperitivo buffet, which you can avail for as low as €9.

The food is delicious. There is also an extensive menu of specialty drinks. Pop and alternative music is the jive in this warm and welcoming eating and drinking place. The crowd is a mix of local and foreign. The age group is between 20s and 30s. It is a perfect spot to start a night of fun in this glorious city.

The bar is located in the neighborhood of Piazza Beccaria, along Viale Antonio Gramsci. Cocktail prices are between €6 and €8. Beer and wine are around €5.

Address:Viale Antonio Gramsci, 1/5 R
Phone:+39 055 234 3890
Kitsch Website
https://www.facebook.com/kitschfirenze/
Kitsch Map
https://goo.gl/maps/i6RcJ75g7R12

Tenax

This night hotspot boasts of the best club music produced by various renowned DJs that come to Tenax by invitation. Great dance music, exquisite drinks and an eclectic crowd is the recipe for good fun. Show off your best moves and enjoy the music with a group of friends.

Tenax is found in the city center. It is also a stone's throw away from other clubs. Although it can be a bit pricey, it is worth the expense if you are looking for a good party.

Address:Via Pratese, 46
Phone:+39 055 308160
Tenax Website
https://www.facebook.com/TenaxOfficialPage/
Tenax Map
https://goo.gl/maps/kzMGHVBDkeL2

Le Volpi e l'Uva

If you want a more quiet way to spend the night, enjoy a glass of exquisite Italian wine at this bar. This is the place where you will find the best wine bar in all of Florence. It is located at Piazza dei Rossi, a short distance away from Ponte Vecchio. There is a wide selection of Italian wines, which you can avail by the glass or by the bottle.

Surprisingly, the prices of their wine list are quite reasonable. For instance, a glass of wine starts at €2.50. You can enjoy a glass of excellent wine with gourmet panini and other delightful nibbles. Le Volpi e l'Uva is open daily from 11am to 9pm.

Address:Piazza dei Rossi, 1R
Phone:+39 055 239 8132
Le Volpi e l'Uva Website
http://www.levolpieluva.com/Le_volpi/Prima_en.html
Le Volpi e l'Uva Map
https://goo.gl/maps/aSVGTPob3hv

Red Garter

This Bar may not have access to the coolest DJs like Tenax does but they do makeup with their exciting themed nights. There is always something new to experience at Red Garter which is why the place is always crowded.

Foreign students and locals alike hang out here, if not for the delicious drink options then to sing to their heart's content during karaoke nights. For the peeps who want to bust a move, there's a roomy dance floor big enough for a crowd. People flock in to the Red Garter especially during the holidays because this club is known for hosting the best events of the season. Their motto here is go all out or go home!

Address:Via de' Benci, 33/r
Phone:+39 055 248 0909
Red Garter Website
http://redgarteritaly.com/
Red Garter Map
https://goo.gl/maps/a7Pu5DdaKG92

Popcafé

Offering a stunning view of the Santo Spirito while you enjoy your well-mixed cocktail in a vintage-inspired setting, Popcafé is a perfect place to spend the night or to be your rest stop before you dance your heart out in the next club. The environment inside is just as upbeat as the outdoor seating.

There's a diverse mix of Popcafé customers. People both young and old, foreigners and locals alike find this bar a delight.

Address:Piazza di Santo Spirito, 18
Phone:+39 055 217475
Popcafé Website
http://www.popcafe.it/
Popcafé Map
https://goo.gl/maps/2cdpud1eTjk

Space Electronic Discoteca

While the happy hour starts early elsewhere, Space doesn't come alive until late at night. After having a drink or two from a bar or getting bored from another club, people come in this to dance until dawn. It is a go-to place for foreigners and locals alike. The club features great upbeat music that will make you want to move all night long.

What better way to get people to bust out their moves than fantastic beats and booze. The club also offers great deals particularly on special nights.

Address:Via Palazzuolo, 37
Phone:+39 347 299 3323
Space Electronic Discoteca Website
http://www.spaceclubfirenze.com/
Space Electronic Discoteca Map
https://goo.gl/maps/qEps1oXf6rk

Cabiria

Also located at the Santo Spirito particularly at the northeast corner, Cabiria is an easy-going bar with a colorful atmosphere. It features a creative décor with its Van Gogh-esque shades of yellow and purple. It is a cool vibe that you can enjoy from the inside out to the sprawling patio set up in the piazza with an ambient lighting and comfortable seating.

On weekdays, the bar plays anything from funk, house, hip-hop to drum and bass. On the weekends, there are DJs and live performances, too. The crowd starts piling up as the bar opens for happy hour from 7pm to 9pm. While some only stay for a drink or two, others find plenty of good reasons to stay for the rest of the night.

Address:Piazza di Santo Spirito, 4-red
Phone:+39 055 215732
Cabiria Website
http://www.cafecabiria.com/
Cabiria Map
https://goo.gl/maps/ykDZopEdGAr

Full Up

This is a '70s club and is still quite popular today. If you are a fan of the disco era, this is something you would want to check out while you're in the city. The owners have made a few tweaks to invite younger crowds and they have been successful in doing so.

Located near the Duomo, Full Up is not hard to find. It is among the most unique hotspots in Florence. It's definitely something different from all the other clubs around. You can dance to the beat or hang around and enjoy the music while you are served with delicious cocktails.

Address:Via della Vigna Vecchia, 23-25
Phone:+39 055 293006
Full Up Website
http://www.fullupclub.com/en
Full Up Map

Via della Vigna Vecchia, 23-25

9

Hotels

Vostra casa lontano da casa

Top 5 Affordable Hotels

Since you will only be in Florence for 3 days, the last thing you want is to spend most of it traveling from a far-flung hotel to the city's tourist attractions. So, we prepared for you a list of the best 2- and 3-star hotels right at the heart of the city center. The best part about this list is they are all affordable.

Hotel Alessandra

Located at Borgo Santi Apostoli, this two-star hotel is a 4-minute walk from the Palazzo Vecchio and the Uffizi Gallery. It is in a Florentine-style building that dates as far back as the 1507. It is an elegant hotel with modern rooms furnished with antique furniture, accentuated by parquet floors and luxurious linens. Hotel Alessandra offers modern amenities.

Guests are charmed by the quaint hotel and its topnotch customer service. Some of the rooms have the most stunning views of the Duomo, the Arno and the St. Trinity Bridge, which is beautiful to look at especially at night. Although the city center is busy, the guests of Hotel Alessandra are well rested because of the peaceful and relaxing atmosphere. Room rates for classic double starts at €130 per night.

Address:Borgo Santi Apostoli, 17
Phone:+39 055 283438
Hotel Alessandra Website
http://www.hotelalessandra.com/
Hotel Alessandra Map
https://goo.gl/maps/hj54xBqJD272

Hotel Casci

Found at Via Camillo Benso Cavour, this two-star hotel has a homey vibe. It is housed within a 15th-century palace and there are actually 2 of them. You will be delighted to know that it is only 6 minutes away from the Florence Cathedral and Michaelangelo's David by foot. Access to the train station at Santa Maria Novella is 10 minutes also on foot.

Hotel Casci is truly a family-run hotel with an old world charm. The original fresco ceilings are still intact as well as the maze of carpeted hallways. Aside from its great location and stunning environment, the service is also a sheer delight. The rooms are well maintained and organized. Their room offers vary from single to couple to family/group rooms. Each room has access to special modern amenities. The rate for the double room is between €75 and €110.

Address:Via Camillo Benso Cavour, 13
Phone:+39 055 211686
Hotel Casci Website
http://www.hotelcasci.com/
Hotel Casci Map
https://goo.gl/maps/cshDL5QPJz82

Hotel Davanzati

Located in Via Porta Rossa, Hotel Davanzati is only a 10-minute walk from Palazzo and Ponte Vecchio. It is also 200 yards away from the Duomo and about 50 yards from Signoria Square. Needless to say, Hotel Davanzati is in the heart of the city.

The hotel consists of 19 smoke-free guestrooms within a historical building. In fact, it stands right next to the Davanzati museum, which is the oldest Florentine house in the city. It is an ideal accommodation for couples on a romantic vacation but it is also family-friendly with an in-room child care available. There are single rooms (€82-202/night), classic double rooms (€122-252/night), superior double rooms (€152-332/night) and suites (€182-352/night). These rooms may not be as quite spacious as the ones in luxury hotels but they are clean and comfortable. Each room has an access to modern amenities.

Among the things that guests look forward to at Hotel Davanzati is the happy hour, which happens every evening in the breakfast room and in the lobby between 6:30pm and 7:30pm. It creates a friendly atmosphere among the guests and gives them a chance to mingle as they are treated to a complimentary Chianti red wine, Prosecco wine, Chianti red wine with some nibbles. TripAdvisor gives it a 5 out of 5 score.

Address:Via Porta Rossa, 5
Phone:+39 055 286666
Hotel Davanzati Website
http://www.hoteldavanzati.it/
Hotel Davanzati Map
https://goo.gl/maps/YeEdiR5FTV82

Hotel Rapallo

Found in the heart of the city center, Hotel Rapallo is just a walking distance away from the city's main attractions. It is located in Via S.Caterina d' Alessandria. It is a family-run 3-star hotel. It is known for being spotless and friendly. In fact, they are very friendly that they extend a warm welcome even to pets. The hotel truly has plenty of surprises for their guests from the moment they walk in.

The staff will go out of their way to ensure that you have a lovely stay. In fact, Lorenzo, the owner himself will make sure you receive nothing less than superb attention. The hotel also offers happy hour from 6pm to 9pm where guests will be served with complimentary cocktails, coffee and hors-d'oeuvres at the hotel bar.

The rooms are delightful and relaxing. While the hotel is a few stone throw away from the busy streets of Florence, guests are ensured of a peaceful stay in their soundproofed bedrooms. Room rates at Hotel Rapallo starts at €90.

Address:Via Santa Caterina D'Alessandria, 7

Phone:+39 055 472412
Hotel Rapallo Website
http://www.hotelrapallofirenze.it/en
Hotel Rapallo Map
https://goo.gl/maps/5fQqkZjdfP52

Hotel Universo

This affordable 3-star hotel is located in Piazza Santa Maria Novella. Hotel Universo is a gem. It is conveniently located, only a few minutes' walk from the train station. It has a boutique-like atmosphere, bright and modern but is far more affordable.

What separates this hotel apart from the rest in Florence is its 70s vintage style. From the furniture to the wallpaper, everything has the 70s vibe. You can also avail of a room with a balcony so you can enjoy the evening breeze with a glass of wine with the lively piazza and the stunning Santa Maria Novella church in sight. Their double room rate starts at €90.

Address:Piazza St. Maria Novella, 20
Phone:+39 055 293891
Hotel Universo Website
http://www.hoteluniversoflorence.com/
Hotel Universo Map
https://goo.gl/maps/hTxBoZTP9dT2

10

Restaurants in Florence

Buon Appetito! Top 5 Restaurants in Florence

Italy is not only known for having an Old World vibe. Italians are also very fond of food. Florence does not fall short when it comes to the selection of restaurants. There are literally hundreds in the city. The question is which ones are worth the time and money. We are counting down the top 5 best eating spots in Florence.

Osteria Vini e Vecchi Sapori

Osteria Vini e Vecchi Sapori is at the very heart of the city. A few steps away from Palazzo Vecchio, this restaurant is well loved by tourists and locals alike. In fact, it was voted Travellers' Choice 2012 Winner Restaurant. Italian food guide Il Mangiarozzo also has it at the top of the list.

It is a nice little restaurant with a warm and welcoming atmosphere. The restaurant serves typical Tuscan cuisine. They specialize in simple and traditional dishes and make use of fresh, genuine ingredients. Osteria Vini e Vecchi Sapori also has an excellent selection of wines.

Travelers recommend the duck pappardelle, osso buco with green peas, chicken liver bruschetta, wild boar ragu, pink ravioli, raspberry tiramisu and grappa. For such a great tasting feast and friendly staff, the prices are reasonable. First course meals are priced between €6 and €8 and the main course around €10 to €14. Reservation is required (055 293045). The restaurant is open from Tuesdays to Saturdays from 9am to 11pm. They are also open on Sundays for lunch.

Address:Via dei Magazzini, 3r
Phone:+39 055 293045
Osteria Vini e Vecchi Sapori Map
https://goo.gl/maps/D1ZPivjJFZn

L'Osteria di Giovanni

Another restaurant that you should check out, which won't cost you too much, is L'Osteria di Giovanni owned by a well known family in Florence dining scene. The atmosphere is welcoming. Decorated with fine artwork from local artists and old Florentine furniture pieces, the atmosphere is just as delightful as the food with the high ceilings and soft lights.

The service is friendly and accommodating. The food is just as impeccable. Among the must-try dishes are smoked goose salad, Bistecca alla Fiorentina, which is a five finger high steak served with roast potatoes and the pastas. The Goose Breast Carpaccio, Pappa al Pomodoro, homemade Pici with Sausage and Kale Ragout and Sirloin Steak with Braised Onions and Pesto are also divine. If you are up to trying something different, you can have the braised rabbit in Vernaccia wine with green olives and sautéed greens.

The restaurant is located at Via del Moro. They are open daily for lunch between 12:30pm and 3pm; for dinner between 7pm and 11pm. It will be more convenient to make a reservation, but walk-ins are welcome too. The prices vary but are reasonable. Expect to spend at least €30 or €45. To make a reservation, you can call them at 055 284897.

Address:Via del Moro, 22
Phone:+39 055 284897
L'Osteria di Giovanni Websitee
http://www.osteriadigiovanni.com/
L'Osteria di Giovanni Map
https://goo.gl/maps/m2V2BGyagvE2

Antica Trattoria da Tito dal 1913

This is an old restaurant with a unique vision. True to old traditions, this eating hotspot in Florence offers a short menu. Like the owner says, they want to have few choices with each one absolutely exquisite. It is a casual restaurant with food as its main attraction.

The must-try list includes their homemade French pasta with mushrooms, le pappardelle al cinghiale or wild boar pasta, artisan cheese sourced from Bagno a Ripoli, cabbage and bean soup, pasta with sausage sauce and lardo di Colonatta. Customers also rave about their 3-pound steak cooked to perfection as well as their list of sumptuous traditional Florence desserts especially the soft almond biscotti with sweet Tuscany wine dip, the vin sinto.

Antica Trattoria da Tito is found along Via San Gallo. The restaurant is open from Mondays to Saturdays. Reservations can be made through phone number, 055 472475. The recommended budget is between €35 and €40.

Address:Via S. Gallo, 112/r
Phone:+39 055 472475
Antica Trattoria da Tito dal 1913 Website

http://www.trattoriadatito.it/home.html
Antica Trattoria da Tito dal 1913 Map
https://goo.gl/maps/xJWnQsZHz942

Ristorante Accademia

Conveniently located at the historical Piazza San Marco, Ristorante Accademia is a small restaurant that serves four-course meals. You will be greeted by a welcoming and attentive English speaking staff. They serve the most delightful old fashioned primi, beef fillet with juniper berries, veal steak and stuffed rabbit. They have a charming blackboard for daily specials. They have specific wine listing recommendations for each course, too.

Ristorante Accademia is open daily from 12pm to 3pm for lunch and 7pm to 11pm for dinner. Reservations can be made at phone number 055 217343. Expect to spend at least €20 to €40.

Address:Piazza San Marco, 7
Phone:+39 055 217343
Ristorante Accademia Website
http://www.ristoranteaccademia.it/en/
Ristorante Accademia Map
https://goo.gl/maps/vMx2D8ukkPw

Enoteca Pinchiorri

If you are in the mood for celebration, then it would not hurt to splurge on a 3-star Michelin restaurant. Enoteca Pinchiorri is one in 6 Italian restaurants that has been awarded 3 Michelin stars. It is expensive, but you won't be disappointed. The service is impeccable, the atmosphere is heavenly, and the food is a sheer delight.

The ingredients are locally sourced, and the wine list is extensive. The exquisite wines are from the Tuscan region. Everything works in great harmony. It is a great recipe for an unforgettable experience.

Located along Via Ghibellina, Enoteca Pinchiorri is open for dinner only from Thursday to Saturday. The restaurant also offers a tasting menu with 15 small plates. The price starts at €200 per person. Make a reservation through this number, 055 242757.

Address:Via Ghibellina, 87
Phone:+39 055 242757
Enoteca Pinchiorri Website
http://enotecapinchiorri.it/
Enoteca Pinchiorri Map
https://goo.gl/maps/7nzU9n6zMCo

11

Special Things You can Only Do in Florence

Special Things You can Only Do in Florence

Here's a list of the most unique experiences you can only have in this great city.

Pay your respects to the Shoe Master at Salvatore Ferragamo Museum.

If you are a fan of shoes, you should make time for this museum. Discover the refined craftsmanship of Salvatore Ferragamo.

The museum displays sketches, photographs, books and wooden lasts of various famous feet including those of Audrey Hepburn, Sophia Lauren and Rita Hayworth among menu others. It is open on weekdays during business hours. The entry fee is €5.

Address:Piazza di Santa Trinita, 5
Phone:+39 055 289430
Salvatore Ferragamo Museum Website
http://www.ferragamo.com/museo/en/usa/
Salvatore Ferragamo Museum Map
https://goo.gl/maps/cSh1pwP6UeF2

Have the best Neopolitan pizza at II Pizzaiuolo.

Found along Via dei Macci, II Pizzaiuolo serves the best Neopolitan pizza in Florence. The fun vibe, the friendly staff and the autentic tasting pizza assures a wonderful experience. Because it is quite a popular place, you would want to either arrive early or call for a reservation at 055 241171. The must-try list includes the delightful Caprese drenched in mozzarella, Bomba and margarita pizza. In addition to pizza, II Pizzaiuolo also offers meat, fish and pasta dishes.

Address:Via dei Macci, 113
Phone:+39 055 241171
II Pizzaiuolo Website
http://www.ilpizzaiuolo.it/
II Pizzaiuolo Map
https://goo.gl/maps/QhpoJcCW2TL2

Enjoy a cup of coffee with a stunning view of the Duomo at Caffetteria Le Oblate.

Located a few steps from the train station, Le Oblate is in fact a public library. The caffeteria can be found at the top floor. You'll be welcomed by a covered outdoor terrace where you can marvel at the stunning view of the Duomo.

You can enjoy a cup of coffee in the terrace or among the arches of the magnificent courtyard as the lovely breeze kisses you cheeks. The place also hosts various cultural events and offers free Wi-Fi. While you have an awesome coffee with a scenic view, the prices at Le Oblate are favorable for budget travelers. A cup of lovely coffee on a gorgeous roof top costs less than €2.

Address:Via dell'Oriuolo, 26
Phone:+39 055 263 9685
Caffetteria Le Oblate Map
https://goo.gl/maps/UQ0fG918PCq

Have a decadent experience with the best Gelato in the world at Gelateria La Carraia!

Florence gave birth to gelato and the best in the world is at Gelateria La Carraia. They have the creamiest, most decadent dark chocolate gelatos among others.

The prices of their gelatos are low but are served in generous portions. A small cone, for instance, costs €1 for a single flavor. La Carraia is located at Piazza Nazario Sauro.

Address:Piazza Nazario Sauro, 25-red,
Phone:+39 055 280695
Gelateria La Carraia
http://www.lacarraiagroup.eu/en/index.html
Gelateria La Carraia
https://goo.gl/maps/HhznXpwhWJT2

Visit the houses of great masters of art and literature.

You cannot get any closer to these geniuses than this.

Casa Buonarroti (Michelangelo's house)

You've seen his masterpieces. Do you want to know more about this great sculptor? Fortunately, an extraordinary museum was built in his honor. Among those in display are preparatory models, studies and sketches that give us a hint of this genius' passion about his work.

Address:Via Ghibellina, 70
Phone:+39 055 241752
Casa Buonarroti Website
http://www.casabuonarroti.it/it/
Casa Buonarroti Map
https://goo.gl/maps/bpCixRw1Nc72

Casa di Dante (Dante's House)

Are you a literature geek? Know more about the founder of Italian language, Dante Alighieri and the inspiration behind his literary masterpieces. This is the house where Dante was born and spent most of his life in.

It documents his entire life and his works. Here you will find ancient books of Divina Commedia as well as Dante's illustrations of paradiso and purgatorio among many other fascinating displays.

Address:Via Dante Alighieri, 14
Phone:+39 347 806 0062
Casa di Dante Website
http://www.museocasadidante.it/en/
Casa di Dante Map
https://goo.gl/maps/PFsazUgi3E42

Enjoy aperitivo and party overlooking the breathtaking Piazzale Michelangelo at Flo' Lounge Bar.

Located at the Piazzale Michelangelo, Flo' is the most exclusive club in the city with the most stunning views. If you like dressing up for a fancy night out, you might as well hang out here. You have to be dressed to the nines to get in. If you want to avail of the aperitivo, you have to arrive early. Otherwise, you'd miss the aperitivo offer and you have a slimmer chance of getting in. There's always a long line outside but those who do get in are treated to an amazing buffet, exquisite cocktails and festive music.

The downside is Flo' is only open during the summer and when the summer months come, people flock in. If you like to tour hard and party harder, you may want to consider checking this place out.

Address:Viale Michelangiolo, 82
Phone:+39 055 650791
Flo' Lounge Bar Website
http://www.flofirenze.com/
Flo' Lounge Bar Map
https://goo.gl/maps/TiFjUDWRbE12

Check out the costumes.

Do you fancy yourself a fashionista? Check out the Costume Gallery and discover how women used to dress. The museum also showcases elaborate theater costumes from different eras. Found in the Pitti Palace, the costume gallery is open at different times depending on the month. You can call them at 055 2388713 to inquire about their schedule during your Florence trip. An entry fee of €8.50 includes admittance to the Museo delle Porcellane and Museo degli Argenti.

Address:Piazza de' Pitti, 1
Phone:+39 055 294883
Costume Gallery Map
https://goo.gl/maps/xKFSF9cuYZw

Great Italian food from a stall at Da Nerbone Due.

A stall located in the middle of San Lorenzo Market, Da Nerbone Due serves economical, quick and warm meals for €12 to €15. Among their best are seafood risotto, salted cod, Florentine tripe, mushroom risotto, pappa al pomodoro, beef and potatoes, pasta with duck or deer or wild boar. A glass of Chianti Classico is available for €1.50.

Da Nerbone Due is open from Monday to Saturday until 2pm only.

Address:Piazza del Mercato Centrale, 12 red
Da Nerbone Due Map
https://goo.gl/maps/3A7Neotoiqv

12

A 3-Day Itinerary in Florence

A 3-Day Itinerary in Florence

Not sure where to start? Here are a couple of suggestions for a 3-day trip.

Day One

6am – Breakfast at the Hotel

8am – Head to the Uffizi Gallery

11:30 am – Eat at Osteria Vini e Vecchi Sapori

1:00pm – Enjoy the walk around Piazza della Signoria

1:30pm – Stop by at Dante's House

2:30pm – Head to Pitti Palace and take a tour of the Gallery of Modern Art,
Palatina Gallery, Royal Apartments and museum of your choice (Silver, Porcelain or Carriage museum)

5:00pm – Enjoy the view of the elegant Boboli Garden at Pitti Palace

6:00pm –Have some gelato

6:30pm – Head back to the hotel to freshen up

7:30pm – Head out early to Flo' Lounge Bar to avail of their aperitivo and a
few drinks afterwards

Day Two

6:30am – Breakfast at the Hotel

9:00am – Go to the Museum of "Florence as it was"

10:30am – Go to Academia Gallery

12:00pm – Lunch at Ristorante Accademia

2:00pm – Head to Palazzo Vecchio

4:30pm – Coffee at Caffetteria Le Oblate and enjoy the view of Duomo

5:30pm – Rent a bike to cross the Arno River to Ponte Vecchio

6:00pm – Rest at the Piazzale Michelangelo and watch the sunset

7:00pm – Pizza dinner at Il Pizzaiuolo

8:30pm – Explore Oltrarno, its artisan workshops, wood carvers, goldsmiths, mosaic makers, etc.

10:00pm – Hang out at the Cabiria

Day Three

6:30am – Breakfast at the Hotel

8:00am – Museo Nazionale del Bargello

10:00am – Museo Leonardo da Vinci

11:30am – Piazza Santa Trínita for luxury shopping

1:00pm – Quick lunch at Da Nerbone Due in San Lorenzo market

1:45pm – Bargain shopping at San Lorenzo

4:00pm – Eat Panino con Lampredotto from a stall in the market

4:30pm – Coffee and bombolini at La Loggia

6:00pm – Head back to the hotel to freshen up for dinner

7:00pm – Dinner at L'Osteria di Giovanni

9:00pm – Drinks at Le Volpi e l'Uva

10:00pm – Head to Full Up

Cut the lines at the city's main attractions by buying your museum and gallery tickets in advance. Spend less time waiting in line and more time exploring!

A 3-DAY ITINERARY IN FLORENCE

13

Conclusion

I want to thank you for reading this book! I sincerely hope that you received value from it!

If you received value from this book, I want to ask you for a favour.Would you be kind enough to leave a review for this book on Amazon?

THANK YOU

CHECK OUT MY OTHER BOOKS !!

https://www.amazon.com/Venice-Short-Travel-Guide-Guides-ebook/dp/B00ON3KZLE/

https://www.amazon.com/Lisbon-Short-Travel-Portugal-Guides-ebook/dp/B018GH4OYQ/

accounting, officially permitted, or otherwise, qualified services. If advice is necessary, legal or professional, a practiced individual in the profession should be ordered.

– From a Declaration of Principles which was accepted and approved equally by a Committee of the American Bar Association and a Committee of Publishers and Associations.

62564197R00046

Made in the USA
Middletown, DE
24 January 2018